Schappi

Anna Haifisch

The Hall of the Brightest Wings

The Mouseglass

A Proud Race

Fuji-San

Letter to Weasel

5 Short Stories

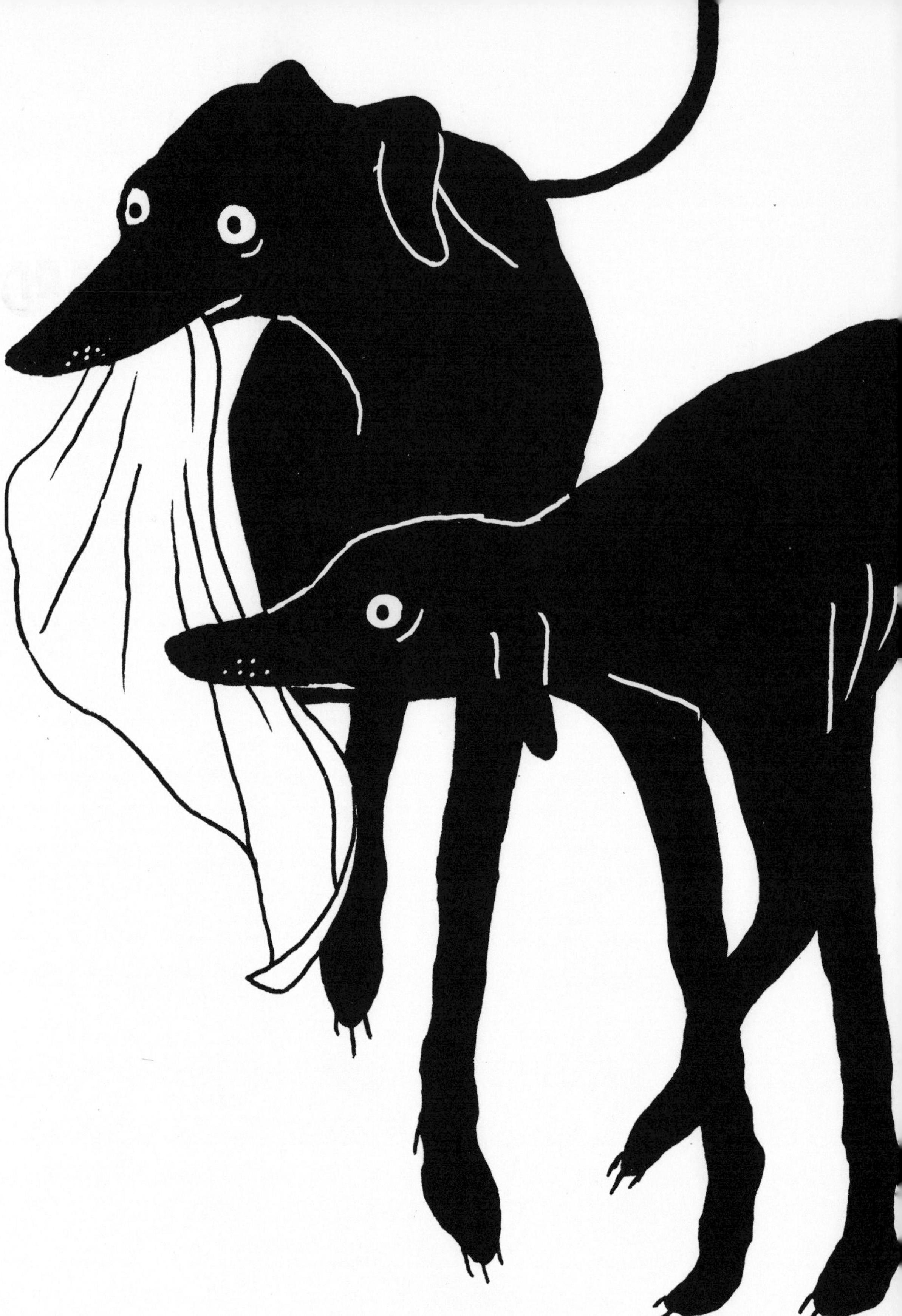

A heart
covered in fur and feathers

A throb
in a meager chest

A friend
with a beak or snout

At home or far away
Baron Vogelfrei and Prince Schappi

My hands are long, my fingers are royal. It has been well documented before. My other body parts are well-shaped, too. I am healthy. I am influential and at last I am very, very rich.

I own a piece of land, on which I erected my gallery. Perhaps I am being too humble.
More accurately it could be described as a great hall for the arts.

Over the years a colony of artists have settled down at the foot of my monstrosity.
Pitiful and droll figures.

There is indeed a reason for them being here. Once a year, on July 1st, upon my request each artist carries their best piece across the ramparts into my hall where I pick three extraordinary pieces for my pristine collection.

The process of creating these works is excruciating. Through my binoculars I've witnessed a few poor souls drowning themselves in the creek behind their cabins and yurts.

They've carved out a grudging and sinister society in which the daily routine is characterized by distrust and mental breakdowns.

It is a bleak sight for me. My binoculars stay in its little velvet casket most of the time.

I have seen it all: Ridiculous sculptures that left an unappetizing, sticky puddle on my parquet floor; strange, awkward paintings; malformed carvings and demented video works.
All of which amounts to little more than a cry for help.

But among the endless stream of drivel I always select three suitable pieces for my noble collection.

The unchosen works of art are burnt immediately under the western balcony.
The fire lasts for six days.

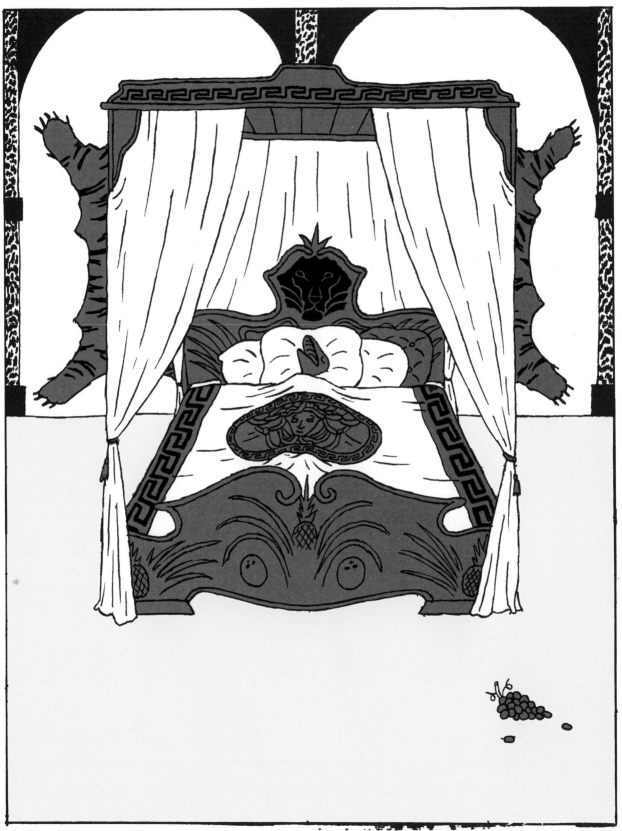

I can hear the artists crying in the distance. The sound lulls me into a deep slumber.

As I rise in the morning, I love to wander through my silent hall.
Every now and then I stop to sweep the dust off of my precious possessions.

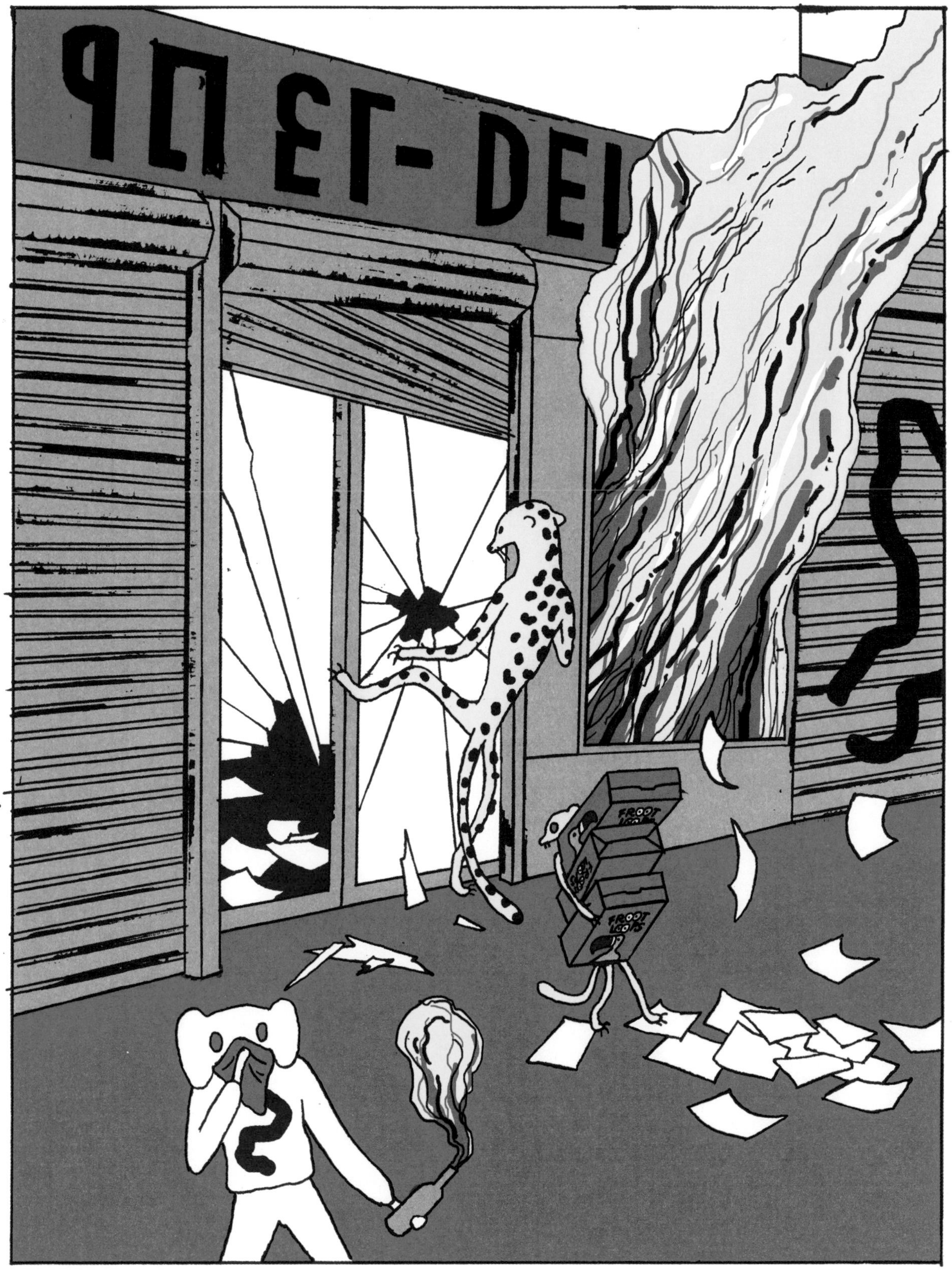
FROOT LOOPS
FROOT LOOPS

The Mouseglass

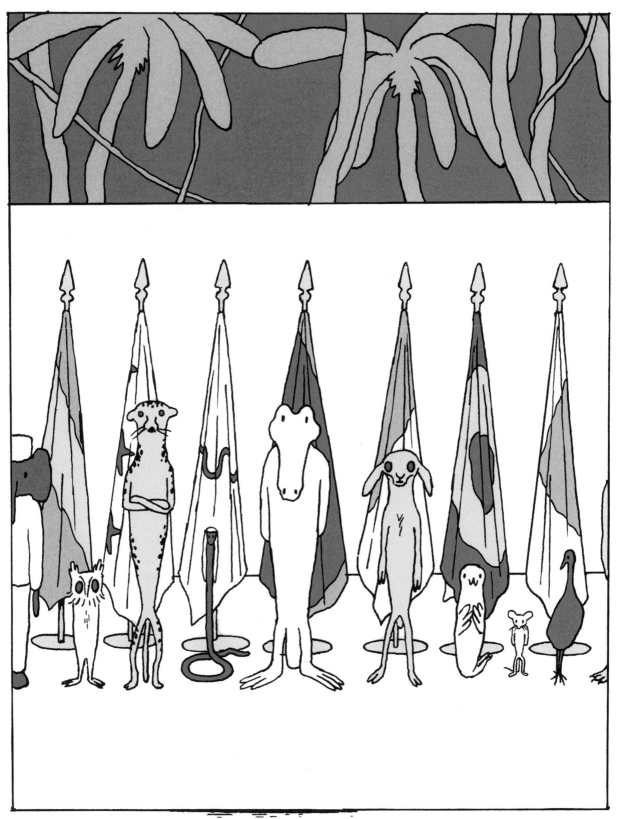

On June 9, 2018, the 42nd animal summit was held in the Elephants' province due to its natural beauty and security. As a community of shared values, the participants take the responsibility to work towards establishing peace and prosperity among the union of species very seriously. Besides their differences the delegates are hoping for meaningful discussions and excellent snacks in a tasteful ambience.

The first to arrive was the Snake sultan and his entourage. Countless servants and 20 cooks. 15 chefs specialized in *haute rodent cuisine*, three snakes responsible for the fruit platters, and seven tea cooks devoted to the Snake emperor's afternoon first flush darjeeling.

His throne was carried in his yurt, along with his and the Snake princess's possessions. As a symbolic gesture of serpent pride, the citizens of the Snake kingdom pitched tents behind the *Chateau Roi Phillipe Baton-Rouellefort,* where the summit was held.

What a merry and warm welcome it was when the others – presidents, kings, delegates, attachés, and ambassadors – arrived on this warm Saturday morning.

The Duck hugged the Snake. The Weasel kissed the Ferret. The Skunk held the Squid's hand for a little too long. The Crocodile fist-bumped Tsar Leopard and the Mouse fun-saluted the Elephant. "Oh you," the Elephant responded coquettishly.

Chattering and chuckling, the animals stepped inside to take their seats. Their eyes glanced in curiosity at what this summit held in store for them. The host welcomed everybody with cordial words and soon the meeting began.

The confederation of amphibians and reptiles promoted a union that expands to the forests and prairies. "A wonderful idea, but the cultural differences are too big to overcome," the mammals and birds agreed.

"Bloated bureaucracy and a sluggish administration will be the result," the Owl snootily noted, "and besides that: Nobody wants to deal with the strictly religious Salamanders. Ticking time bombs are what they are." "Faggot!" thought the Duck and reached out for another canapé. She smeared the caviar under the Sloth's iPad.

The Crocodile excused himself to use the bathroom and snuck out to relax a little bit in his suite.

The Weasel, no taller than a toilet brush, talked hectically about inheritance taxes. The Goat interrupted her: "That Ferret matter doesn't bring anyone present in this room any further. You save that topic for your little Ferret parliament." And here the jolly atmosphere soured. "We are Weasels, Ferrets are communists by definition, they don't own commodities..." the Weasel whimpered and teared up. Ferrets, Weasels, Martens... they all look the same to the Goat.

That moist Weasel provoked the Snake princess's swallowing reflex. She cleared her throat and held up her glass for a refill to quench her compulsion.

During tea time, the animals wandered in small groups through the pleasure garden, or gathered on the terrace to revel in light conversation. First husbands and wives joined their spouses and soon happy laughter mixed with exquisite cigar smoke that rose from the crowd. At 3:30PM everybody picked a last scone and returned to their seat.

Next was the Hyena, begging for sustainable investments in her region. She earned pitiful glances and restrained coughs. With her bald patches, feverish eyes, and bleeding gums, she clearly resembled the bottom drawer mammal of the whole summit. "Hyenas are such downers! But news flash," the Mouse whispered to the Crocodile, "you eat diseased and maggot-infested cadavers all day long and you get ill." And with that said he raised his hand.

"I pursued the development in the Hyena region with great concern over the past couple of years. My country's possibilities, and dare I speak for everybody in this room, are exhausted. The motifs of such unpleasantness remain unclear to me and my folks but I'd rather cut ties here and today before I spend a single dime on development aid for a nation of degenerates." The Mouse squinted in the direction of the Hyena. "When did the Mouse become so racist?" the Crocodile thought.

"How does the united community of animals intend to deal with such disheveled laziness in the future?" "What is it with those rodents?" the Crocodile pondered. "Isn't it funny how a certain kind of species can stink up the whole atmosphere?" the Mouse laughed. That was when the hog-nosed Skunk left the room.

"To hell with stink bears," the Falcon croaked. The Mouse nodded in compliance and just as he was about to raise his tiny little hand again, the Crocodile put his juice glass over this funky fellow and muted his squeaky voice.

He pressed the glass down a little harder, for three more minutes, and was surprised to find the little loudmouth unconscious under his glass. When he touched his meager chest, the Crocodile realized that the Mouse president was as dead as a door nail.

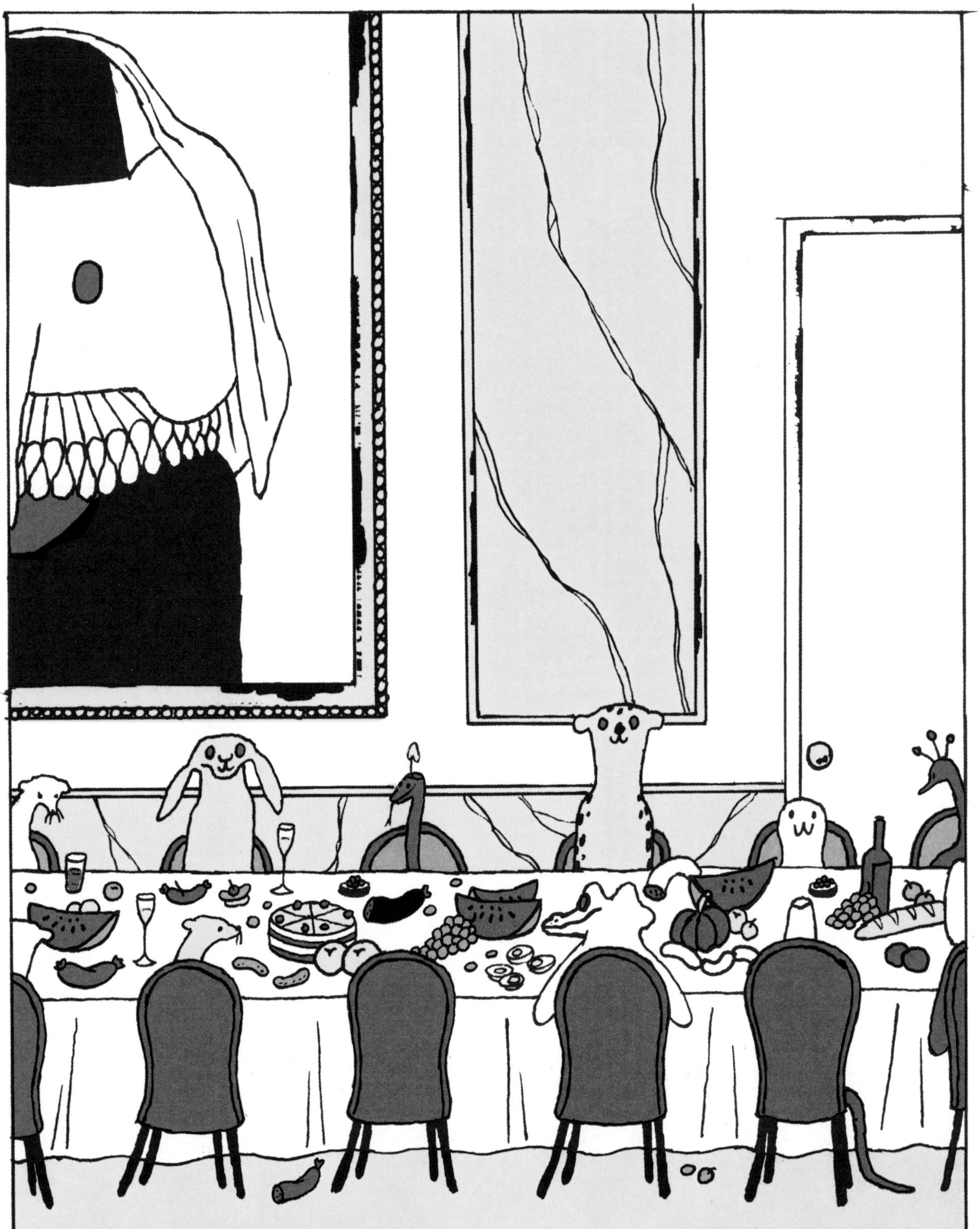

The Snake princess across the table couldn't take her eyes off the Weasel delegation. After two noisy gulps from her direction, the solution of the Mouse problem dawned on the Crocodile. He wrapped up the Mouse carcass in his napkin and secretly handed it over to the Snake with a wink: "A little souvenir from the Nile."

The Snake pretended to scratch the tip of her tail under the table and disappeared with her warm present for a second or two. Two thankful yellow eyes blazed from across the table and it was at that moment that the Crocodile became aware of how pretty she was. He wondered if he could ever fall for a Snake.

A handful of topics remained unresolved. What about the riots in the deep sea, with an imminent civil war around the corner?

"None of our business," stated the Falcon. "Since the fish couldn't be bothered to come make their case, the animal community shouldn't waste any time with this affair. Our oxygen doesn't seem to be good enough for those slimy lads, huh?" You think Falcon and you automatically think: sharp! But that surely doesn't apply to this delegate.

What about women's rights and legal abortions in the Rabbit community? The mining disaster in the republic of the Moles? The Cricket refugee crisis? "What's for dinner?" the Elephant asked and called it a day.

The animals happily proceeded towards the dining hall. Appetizing sushi creations dazed their shy eyes. The Goat admired the ice swan a little too much, in the Weasel's opinion. She carved the word "Asshamster!" into the sculpture.

The Falcon released a mean tweet between two california rolls and fell asleep on his Blackberry. Indeed, it was a busy day.

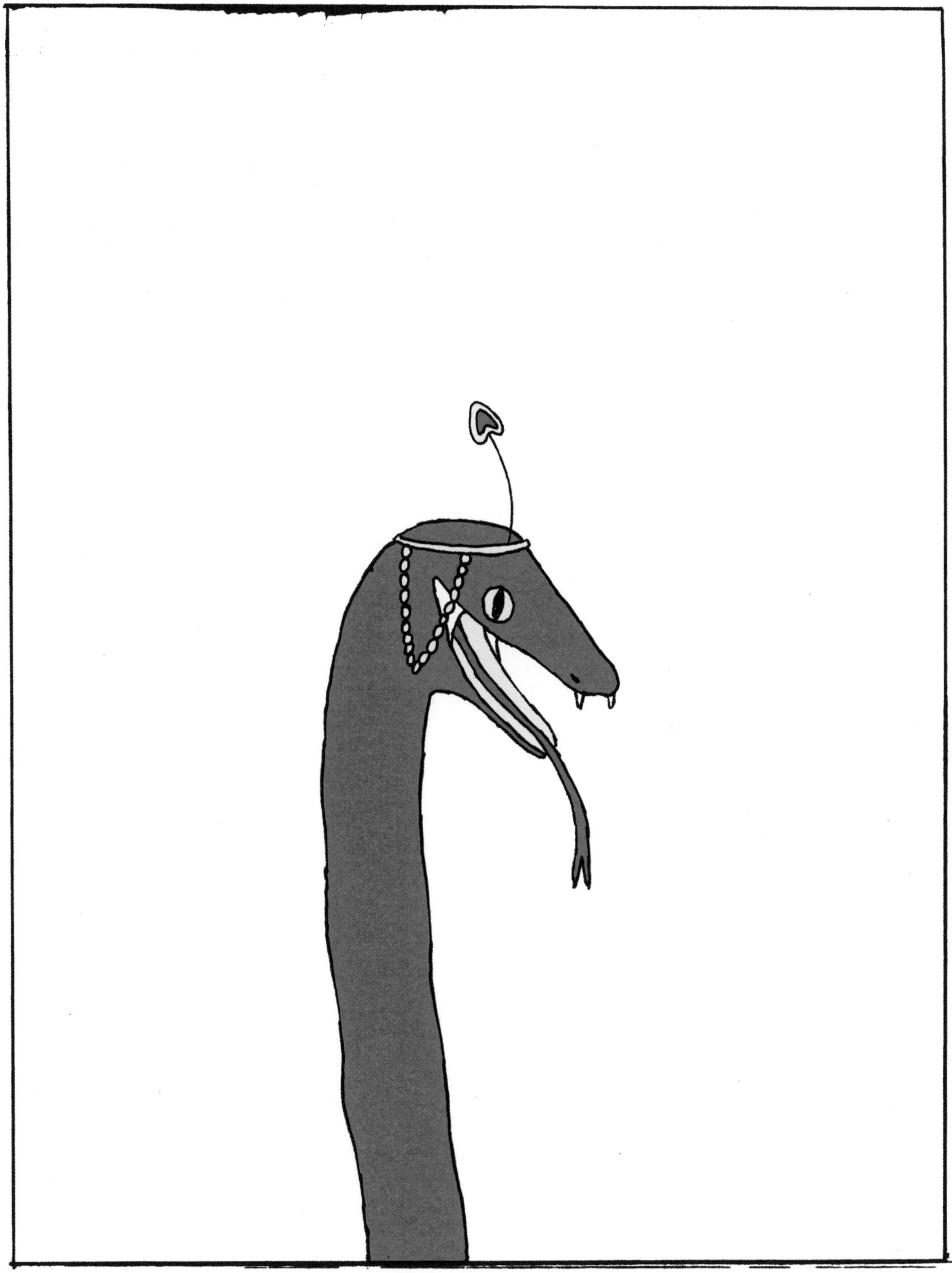

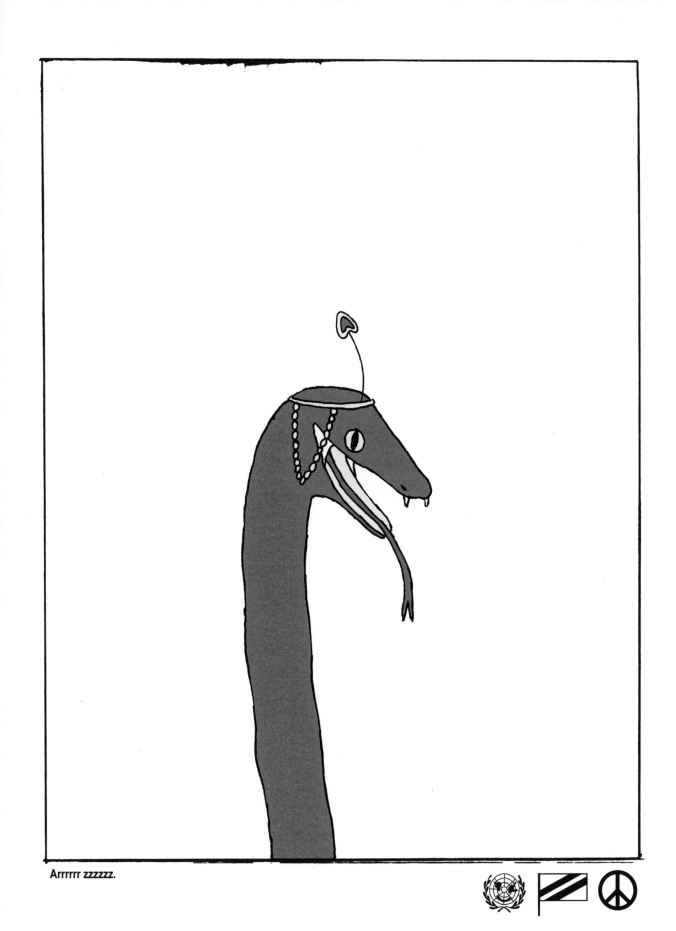

Arrrrrr zzzzzz.

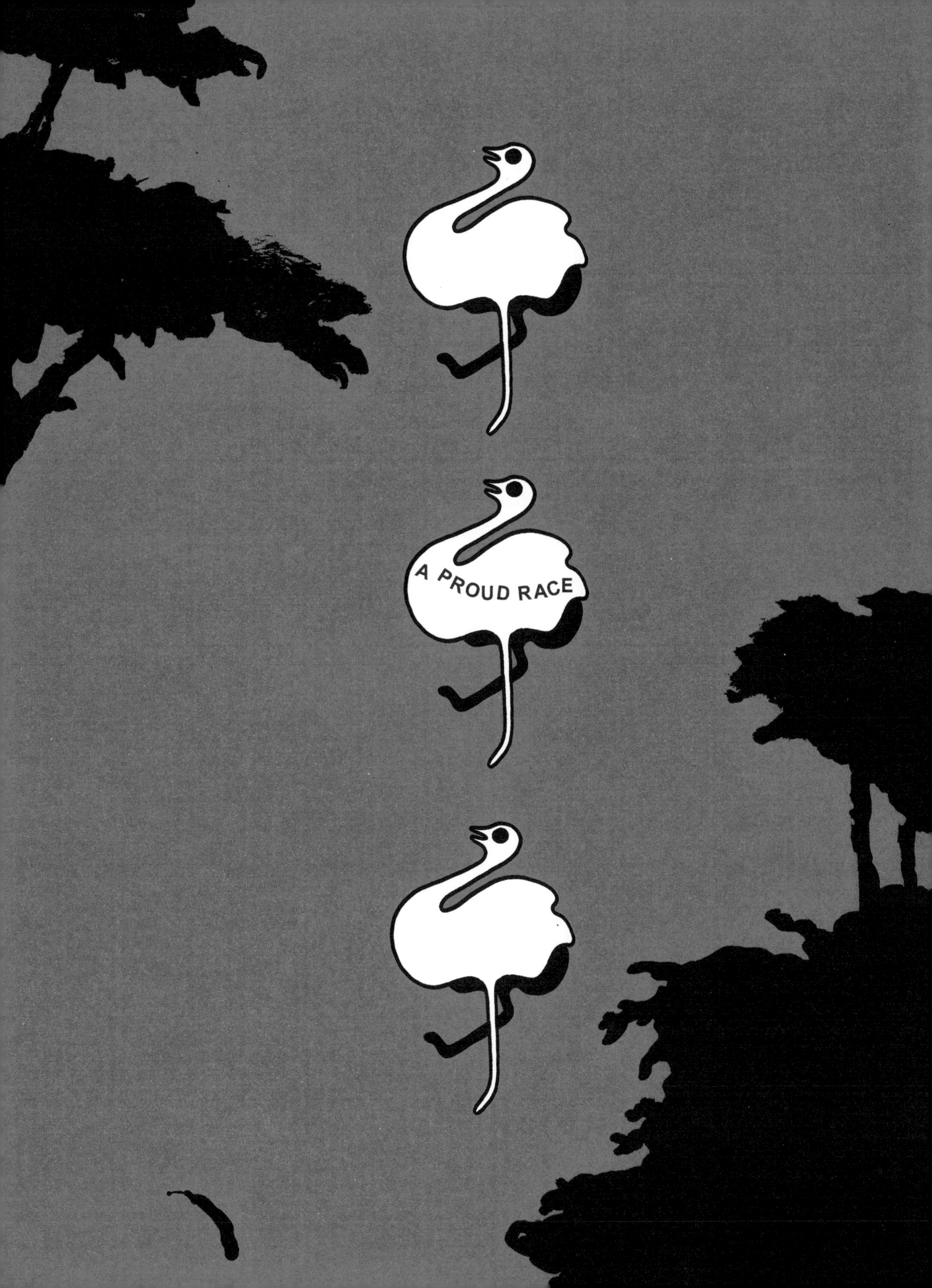
A PROUD RACE

MARCEL WAS A WONDERFUL RUNNER.

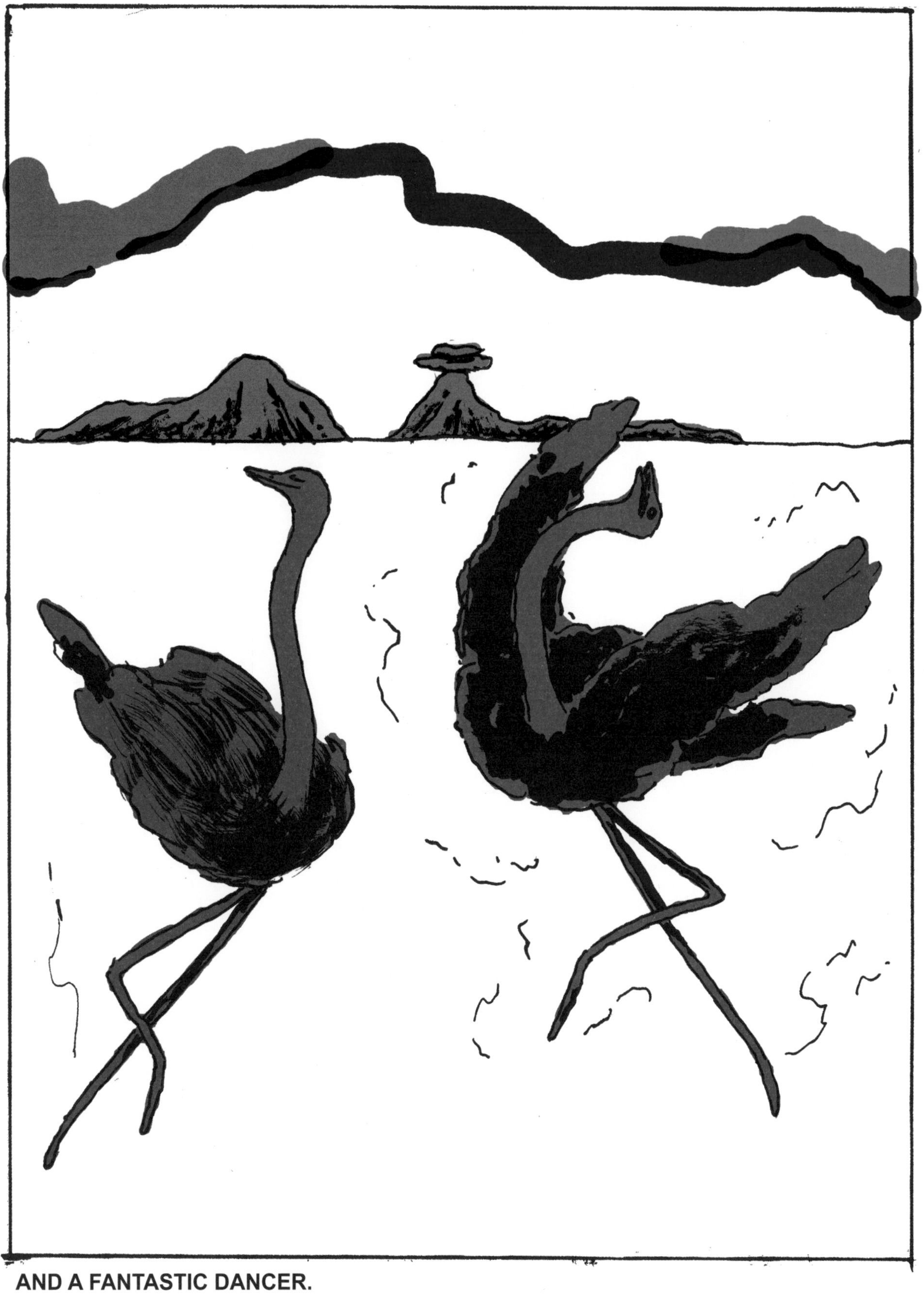

AND A FANTASTIC DANCER.

OOOH, HOW MUCH I LOVE RUNNING IN OUR GROUP.

MARCEL, MINNIE, BEAK BENNY, MOHAMMED JR., HOLLY, J. CARLOS, BROOKE,
ALISTAIR, HUGO, WILMA K., ELEANOR, AND ME.

DASHING IN SYNC. IMPERIAL AND PROUD, OR EVEN... DARE I SAY...

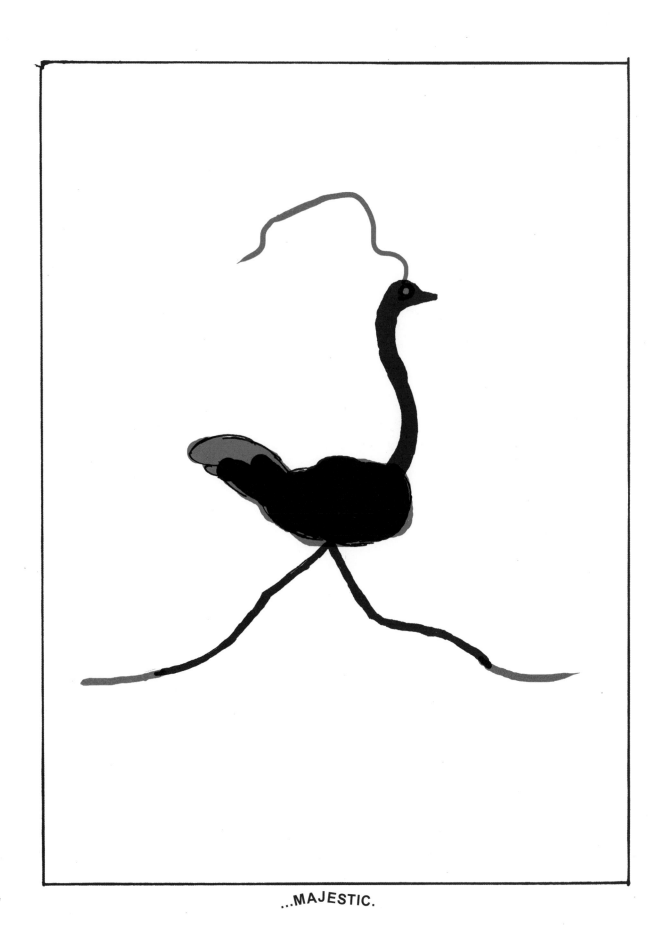

...MAJESTIC.

ELEANOR IS MARCEL'S FAVORITE HEN. A GORGEOUS BIRD.
SAMSUNG CASTED HER RIGHT OFF THE OPEN PLAI...

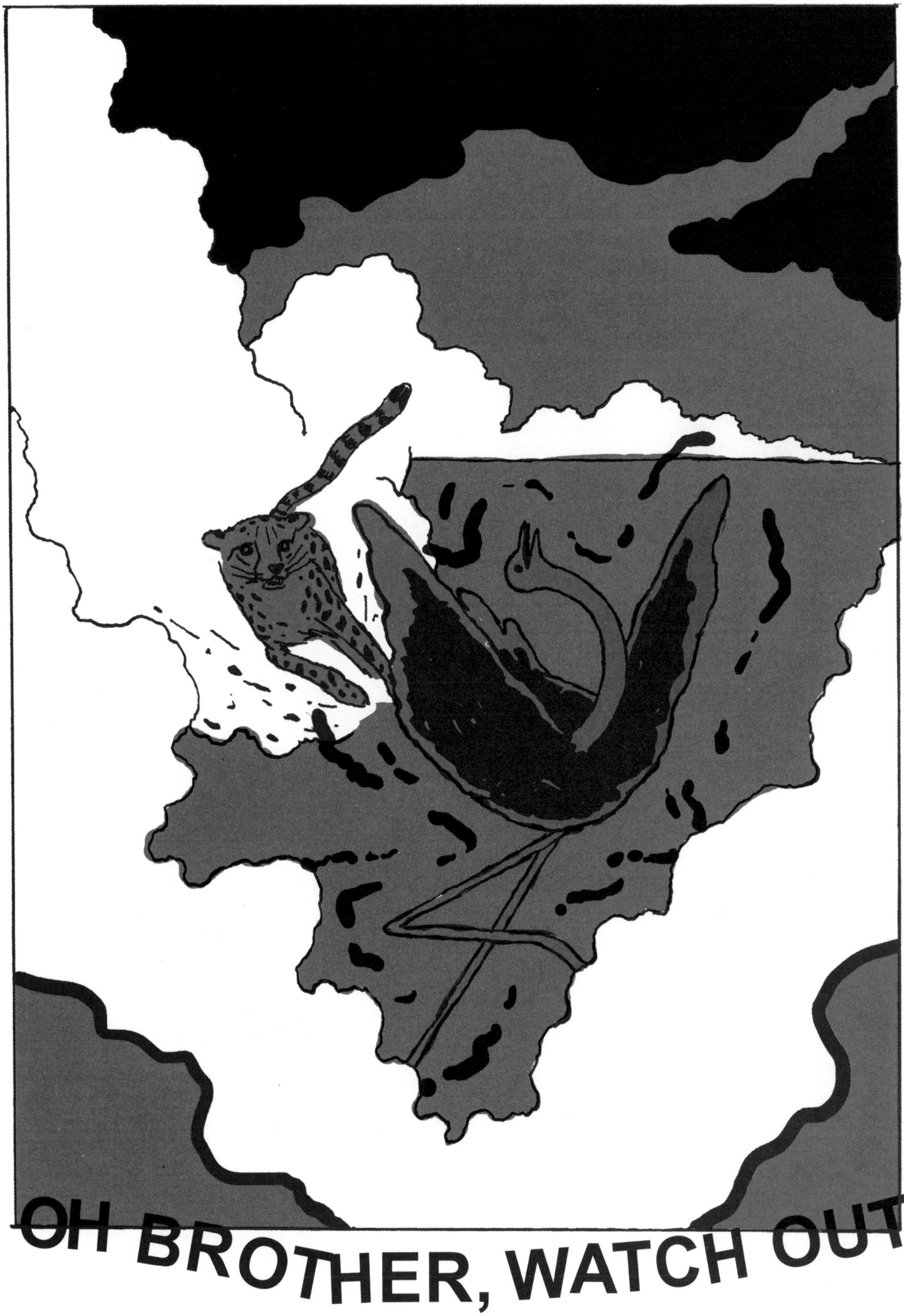

OH BROTHER, WATCH OUT!

FAREWELL, SWEET MOHAMMED JR.

WE DON'T CRY OVER SPILT MILK.

WE HONORED MOHAMMED'S NOBLE DEATH BY RUNNING IN FORMATION.
AND MARCEL DID THAT SEXY DANCE AGAIN LATER THAT NIGHT.

富士山
FUJI-SAN

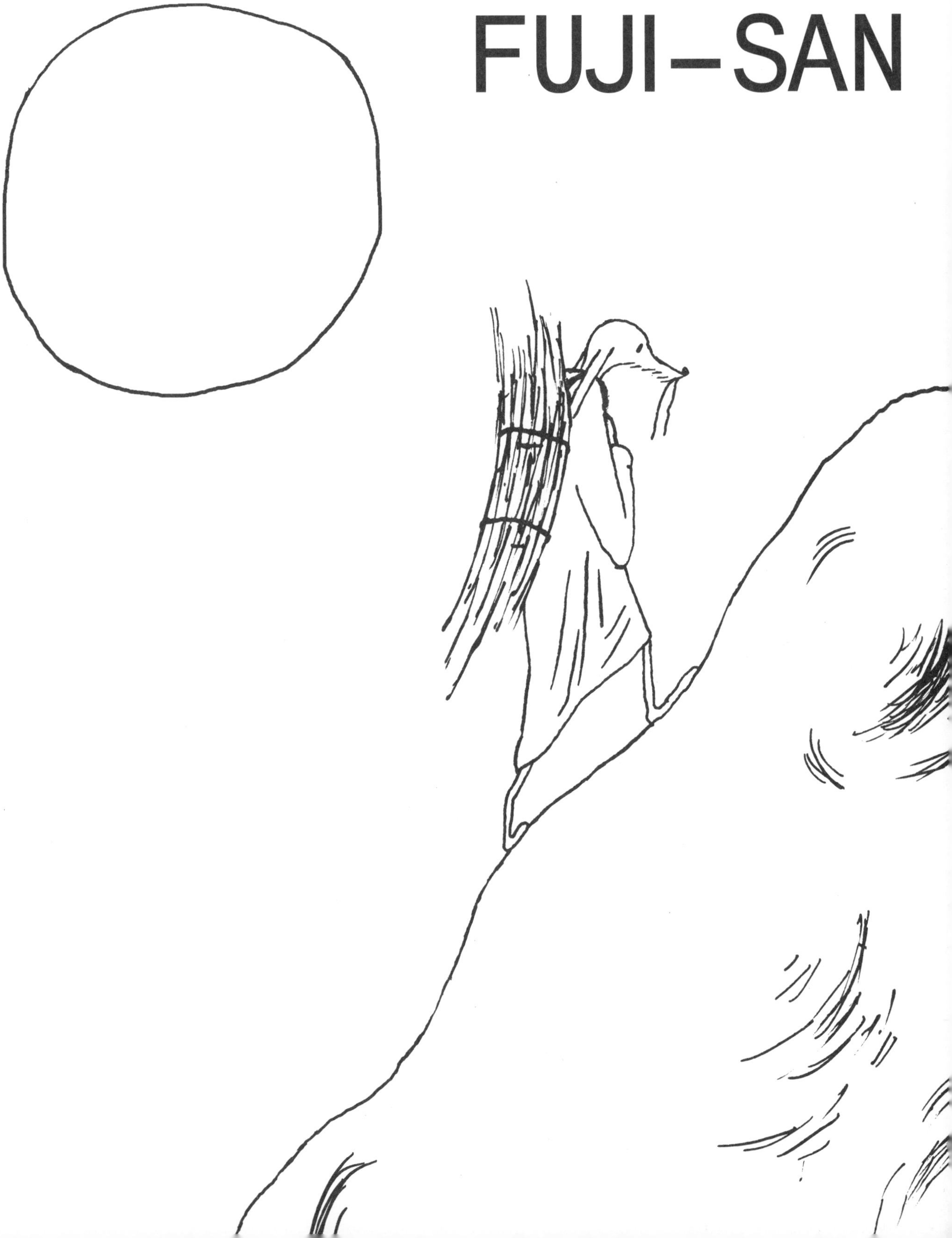

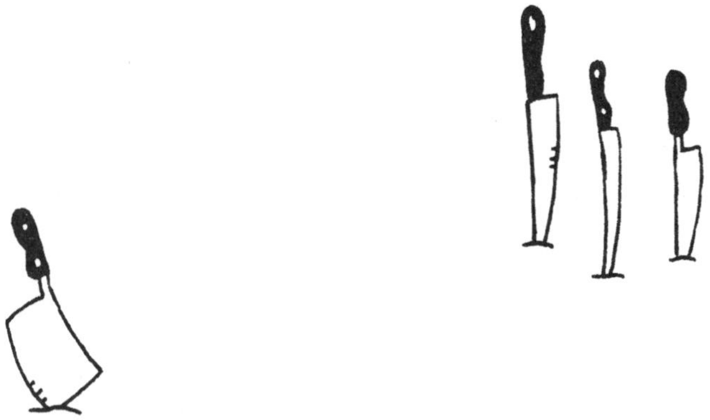

After a venturesome life I settled down   at the foot of Mount Fuji.

Earlier I folded some origami for a   little bit and drew a picture.
   My vase served   as a model. I grew fond of this drawing even though
it's not my best.

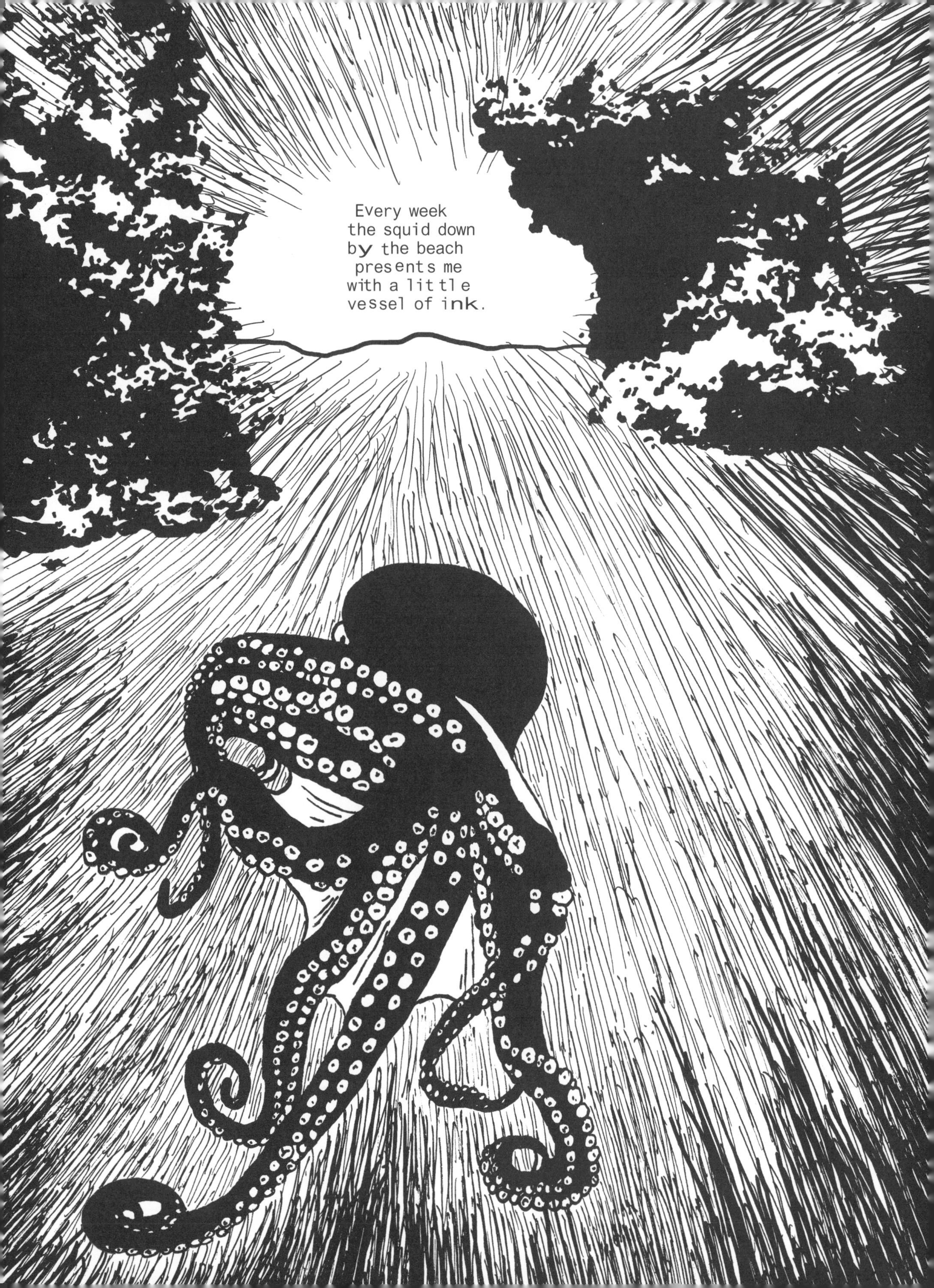
Every week the squid down by the beach presents me with a little vessel of ink.

Therefore I'm very thankful and built him little friends made of udon noodles.
Since I got to KNOw him, I unlearned the word loneliness.   He can't speak
yet we're having very stimulating conversations.
He's the most pleasant company.

Very recently   his wife got
caught and was killed. That made
him bitter. He cried black ink
tears for 41 days straight. I fed
him with soft-boiled
  vegetables and rice balls.
    (I'm an awful cook.)

Unfortunately, the squid and I can't visit each other. He would dehydrate in my house and I wouldn't find my way around his slippery home.

When the squid fancies it, we're playing dominoes in the evening down by the beach. He is a remarkably cunning player who knows to play his stones diligently. Often, however, he underestimates my mental prowess and keen foresight.

The other day I found myself at the sidelines of a cock fight behind the Soba fields. What a vicious spectacle !

When it was over, I took one **of**   the badly injured   roosters home   with me.
I thought he could be a companion and I could t r a i n h i m **a** little   bit.

Now he is
silently
  picking
corn in front
of my house.
Som etimes
I see him
playing with
a wOrm.
That is a
very hopeful
sight.

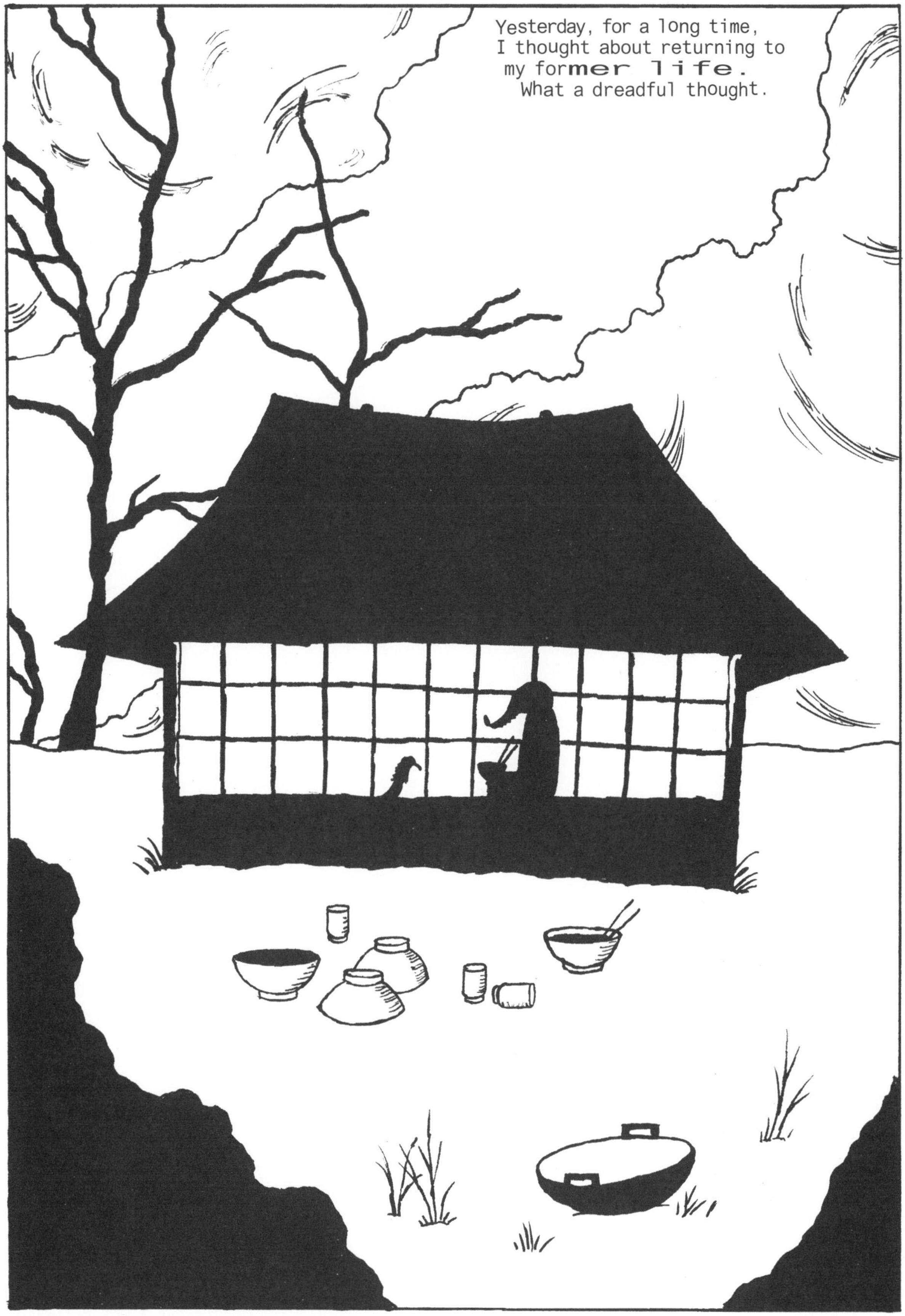
Yesterday, for a long time, I thought about returning to my former life. What a dreadful thought.

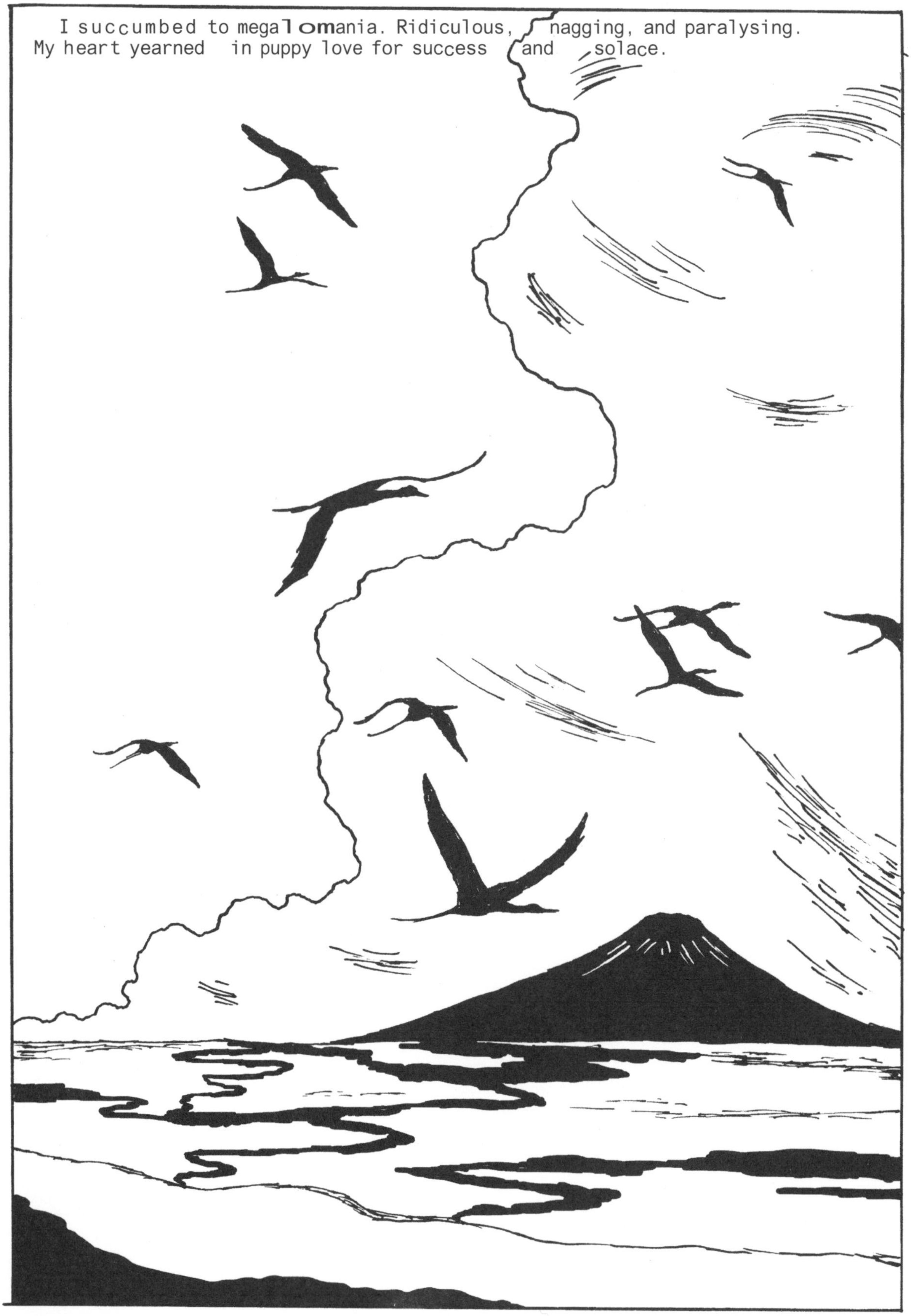
I succumbed to megalomania. Ridiculous, nagging, and paralysing.
My heart yearned in puppy love for success and solace.

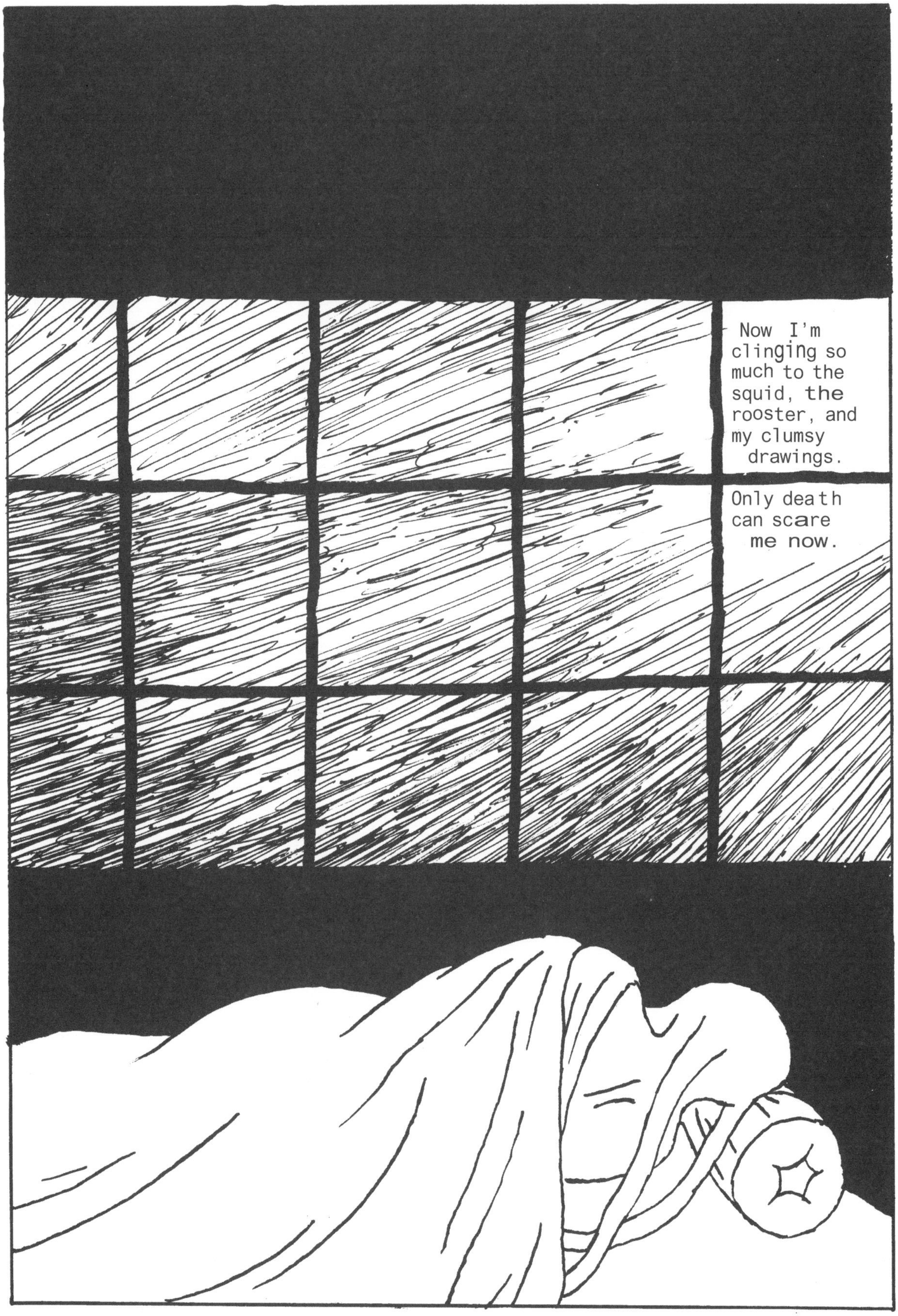
Now I'm clinging so much to the squid, the rooster, and my clumsy drawings.
Only death can scare me now.

the rabbit's poem

Fuji-San stand by me
please don't abandon us.
Squid, rooster, and I —
  we cherish you.

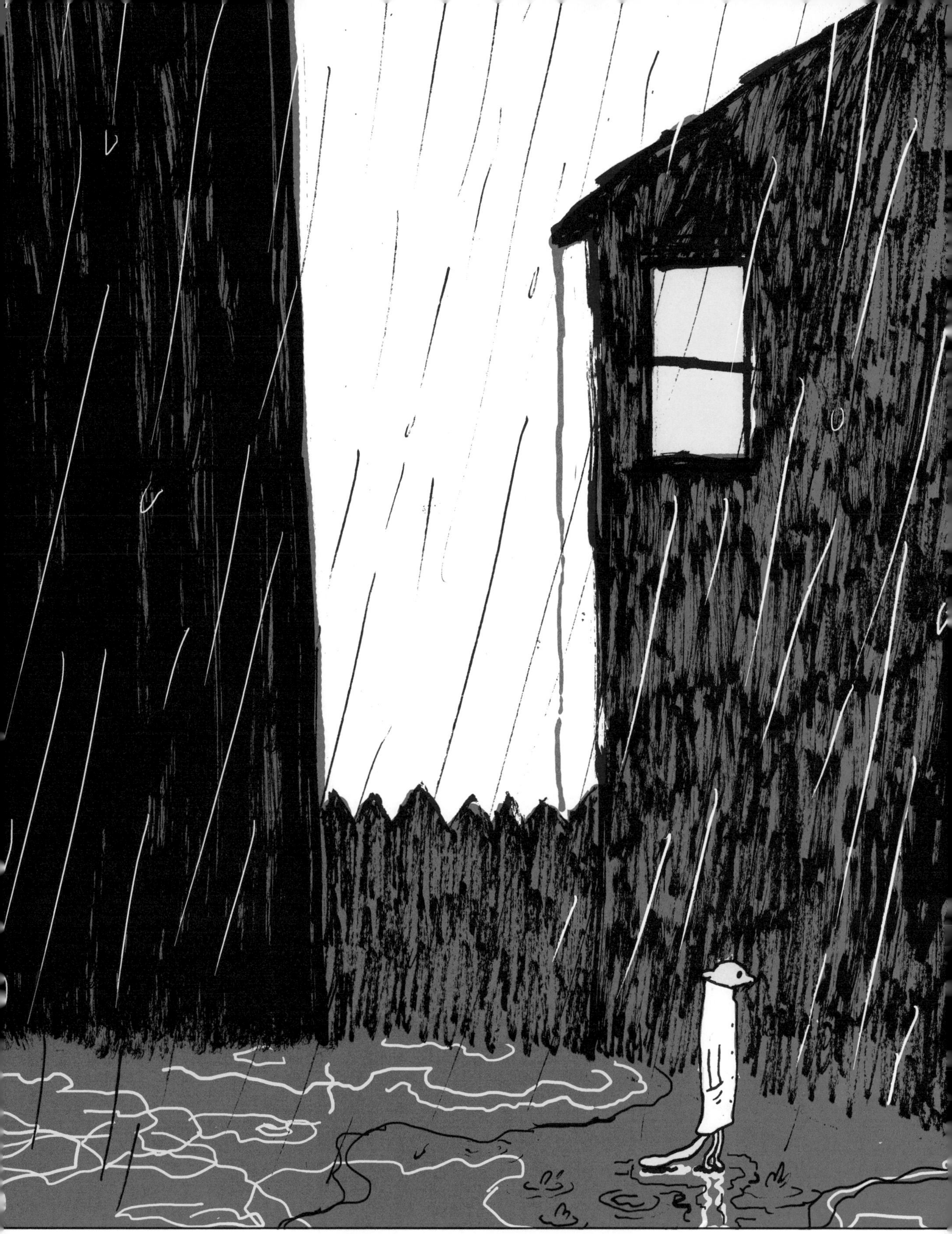

Letter to Weasel

The Weasel felt sick on the bus and later sat in a spit-covered bus shelter near the little tree stump for 22 minutes. Waiting for the connection. Maybe something was wrong with the fruit puree at the *Half-King Cafe*.

The Weasel felt miserable and cold in its thin coat. It pulled its legs closer to the body and thought of a failed meeting with the editor of the local newspaper.

That there isn't any interest in the comics the Weasel drew after work was obvious 10 minutes into the meeting.

Out of insecurity, the Weasel ordered a big bowl of fruit puree and a whole bottle of mineral water. It didn't want to appear poor in front of the editor.

The big portions prolonged the meeting unpleasantly. In front of his empty latte the editor talked about a research trip to the Gobi Desert and folded a swan out of his napkin.

The Weasel stared at the billboard and thought for no reason
of its apartment.

After all I live in a house with lots of young people. The Otter is really friendly. And the Guinea Pig community is also ok, it thought. I should organize my flat more maturely. Towels of the same color and maybe a metal shelf.

When the bus came, the Weasel used the back door because its ticket expired. It started to drizzle.

The bus passed the one and only gallery in the city. The gallerist, a tall Rooster, had AIDS. Everybody in the city knew that. *The only one I know with AIDS,* thought the Weasel. *That makes the Rooster very* *metropolitan. Rooster of the world. With HIV one has an average life span nowadays,* thought the Weasel and almost admired the Rooster for its illness.

Fox Plaza, the Weasel got off and ran home through the rain. The Guniea
community is throwing a party and everybody is invited, read a little note
sted in the stairwell.

The Weasel looked into the mailbox and found an eagerly anticipated letter.
With shaking hands, it carried the envelope all the way up the stairs where it lived.

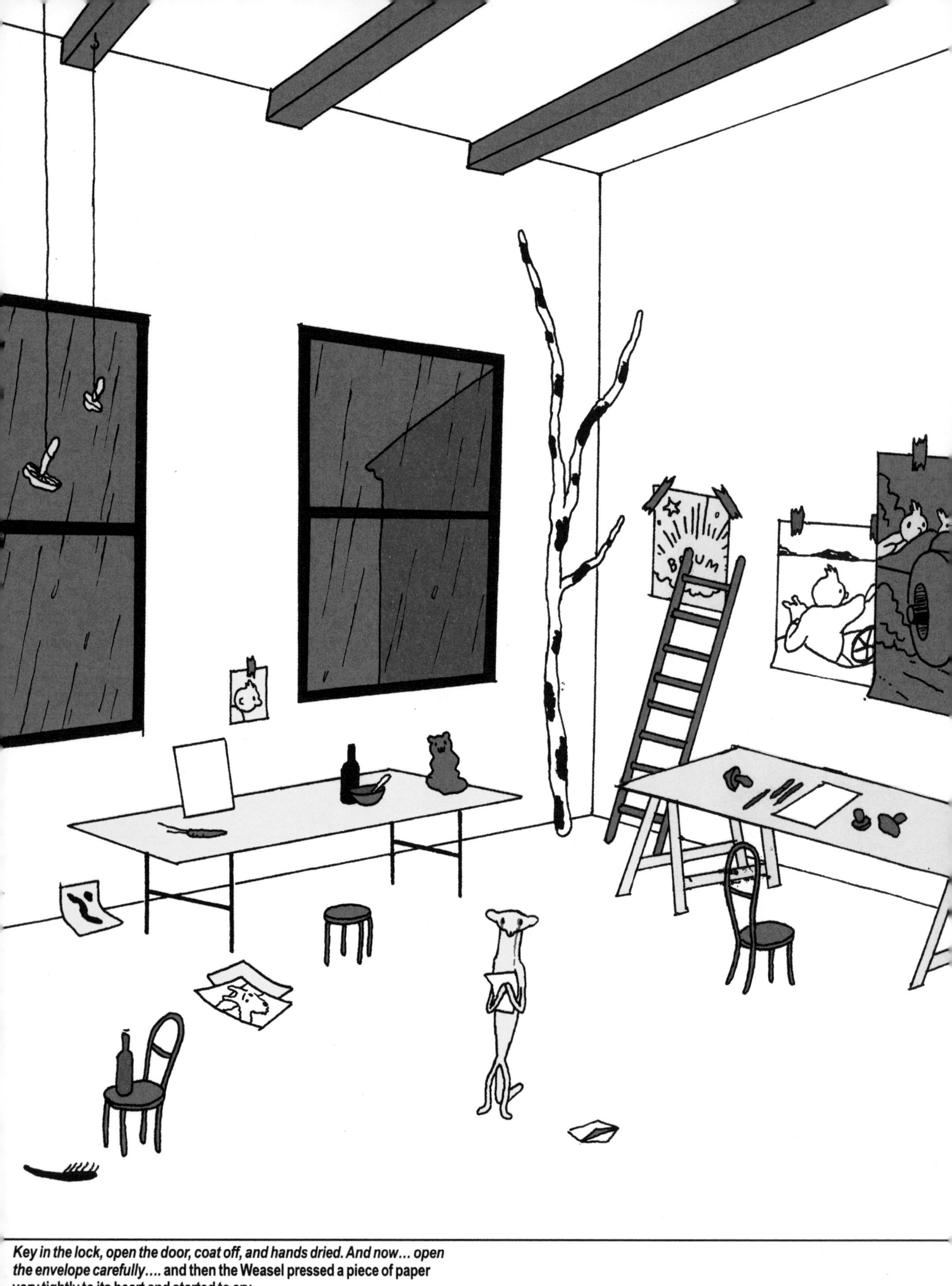

Key in the lock, open the door, coat off, and hands dried. And now... open the envelope carefully.... and then the Weasel pressed a piece of paper very tightly to its heart and started to cry.

Dear Weasel,

Congratulations!
You have demonstrated the admission
requirement and artistic qualification for
the Academy of Visual Arts.
We ask you to pick up your submitted
work samples (portfolio and object made
of stick and glue) from now until April
16th in room 23 on presentation of this
notification. The University reserves the
right to destroy the portfolio and
object if not picked up by the dates
mentioned above.

With kind regards,
Aeni Lizard
Head of the Admission Committee

S c h a p p i

ISBN 978-1-68396-526-8

"The Mouseglass" was originally
published as *The Mouse Glass*
(Perfectly Acceptable Press, 2018).
"A Proud Race" was originally
published in *Now: The New Comics
Anthology* #3 (Fantagraphics, 2018).
"The Hall of the Bright Carvings"
was originally published in
Kramers 10 (Fantagraphics, 2019).

Translation made in
arrangement with Am-Book Inc.
(www.am-book.com).

FANTAGRAPHICS BOOKS INC.
7563 Lake City Way NE
Seattle, WA 98115
www.fantagraphics.com

Editor: Eric Reynolds
Designer: Justin Allan-Spencer and
Anna Haifisch
Production: Paul Baresh
Promotion: Jacquelene Cohen
VP / Associate Publisher: Eric Reynolds
President / Publisher: Gary Groth

ISBN 978-1-68396-526-8
Library of Congress Control Number
2021945391
First printing: April 2022
Printed in China

10 best animals
Heron
Longdog
Ostrich
Crocodile
Snake
Lizard
Elephant
Guinea Pig
Budgie
Long Weasel

Thank You!
Aeni Kaiser
James Turek
Franziska Leiste
Stefanie Leinhos
Rita Fürstenau
Jaqc Cohen
Eric Reynolds
Justin Allan-Spencer
Fantagraphics